A Wild Shining

A Wild Shining

Poems by

Nancy Dillingham

Cover design by Shay Culligan
Cover art by Olga Dorenko
"Purple Phase," oil on canvas www.olgadorenko.com
Author photo by Bill Mosher

ISBN: 978-1-63980-279-1

Kelsay Books
502 South 1040 East, A-119
American Fork, Utah 84003
Kelsaybooks.com

Contents

1.

The Humanity of Birds	13
Uvalde	14
Universal Juror	15
Magdalene Laundries	16
Social Mores: Circa 1950s	17
Jam Up and Honey	18
Before Me Too	19
A Caution	20

2.

A Single Fist	23
Date Night in Ukraine	24
Last Lullaby in Ukraine	25
A Songbird in Ukraine	26
Slava Ukraini!	27
Putin's Stain	28

3.

Alfred Hitchcock: Never Woke	31
Purple Haze	32
Purple Rain: Epitaph for a Prince	33
Mitch	34

4.

A Wild Shining	37
Fossil	38
Democracy	39
Juneteenth	40

Once upon a Time   41
Pandemic: 1918   43
Eastertide: 2021   44
The Poetry of Redwoods   45

I live on a big round ball.
I never do dream I may fall.
—Jesse Winchester

1.

Unable are the loved to die,
for love is immortality.
—Emily Dickinson

The Humanity of Birds

"58 geese gassed in Fairview—by the government?"
—headline, *Asheville Citizen-Times,* 7/18/2021

At the behest of the US government
per the request of the company
near the pond where 58 geese
had taken up residence

a truck arrived from the Department
of Agriculture and Wildlife services
loaded with 2-by-4 yellow plastic crates
massacre and annihilation its purpose

An enforcement officer emerged
grabbed the hapless birds
(who were molting and couldn't fly)
by their wings and necks
and stuffed them in cages

That night the unlucky bystanders
could not unhear the geese's screams
and images of Auschwitz and Dachau
troubled their sleep and dreams

Uvalde

5/24/22

". . . not waving, but drowning."
—Stevie Smith

I see you waving
19 brave 4th and 5th graders
and 2 courageous teachers

Nevaeh, Jackie, Jayce
Jose, Makenna, Ellie
and Irma

Xavier, Uziyah, Amerie
Tess, Maranda, Layla
Alithia, Annabell

Jailah, Rojelio, Maite
Lexi, Eliahana
and Eva

I see you
calling 911
waiting 78 minutes

muzzled by a gunman
unable to shout
bleeding out

not waving
but drowning

Universal Juror

4/21/21

The lawyer
rises

behind
the glass cage

makes
his case

Our mind
races behind

All we can see
are the nine

minutes
and twenty-nine

seconds
of excessive force

applied to the neck
by Chauvin's knee

recorded on her phone
by a seventeen-year-old

hapless bystander
to the crime

Magdalene Laundries

1922–1996

"They like to drive us down the drain."
—Joni Mitchell

As the Sisters of Mercy hurled insults
flogging and beating the young girl
for not completing her chores

blood sullied the nuns' spotless garments
commingled with knotty water
staining red the convent's floor

Social Mores: Circa 1950s

My cousins and I spoke in hushed tones
as we peered at the congregation of convicts
made up mostly of dark faces
working on the road

until Grandma explained that in her day
members of the black race
refused to eat at the dining room table
choosing instead to take their meals

on the small adjoining back porch
knowing their place

Jam Up and Honey

They called my cousin
Jam Up and Honey
his given name James
too straight, not funny

Drove a school bus
he called the "Blue Goose"
loved his uniform
got all gussied up

His nickname came
from a black-face duo
that sang on the radio
on the Grand Ole Opry

On his mama's Victrola
he played her 78's
loved Jimmie Rodgers
and could whistle like a train

I see him now
dipping and bowing
dancing with her
before they took him away

Before Me Too

"A million things you can't have
will fit into a human hand."
—Barbara Kingsolver

Naïve in seventh grade
I watched the ritual
of our teacher standing
in front of the window
his arms draped
around the shoulders
of two of my more
endowed girlfriends
waiting for the second-load
buses to arrive before
classes began

Removed and yearning
cold and lonely
craving attention
wondering how
I could earn it
I watched the wind
blowing like ghosts
over the playground

We all liked the teacher
and missed him
even grieved for him
when he didn't return
to the classroom
the next year

No one bothered
to tell us
why he had to leave

A Caution

"A man has every season
  while a woman only has the right to spring."
                                    —Jane Fonda

At a certain age
she stops meeting

the eyes of young men
on the street

stops admiring
their easy gaits

their wiry bodies
their grace

stops gazing
at her face

annihilates
her smile

chucks the tease
in her voice

holds a funeral
for her youth

a wake
for her fate

imagines
bleeding out

on a *Vanity Fair*
fashion page

2.

Not knowing when the dawn will come
I open up every door.
                    —Emily Dickinson

A Single Fist

When asked
how Ukraine
managed to hold
the capital of Kyiv
while outnumbered
by the Russians tenfold
President Zelensky told
the reporter

We enlisted
the heroism of everyone
the people
the authorities
the armed forces
we united a nation
we fought for our existence
for our survival

we became a single fist

Date Night in Ukraine

It's hard to be
romantic about
starlight that doesn't
shine above you

sleeping on pallets
in overcrowded shelters
crushes of people
around you

It's tough
to think about
the subtleties
of lovemaking

with the stench
of unwashed bodies
surrounding you

But during a hush
between bombs
one young couple
found a way

She gave him
her last, shiny apple
He took a bite
juices running

She lapped it up
savoring it

Last Lullaby in Ukraine

In Memoriam: 3/18/22

109 empty baby
carriages

placed
in central square

draped
in black crepe

accompanied
by guns

and carrion

A Songbird in Ukraine

A songbird sang
in Ukraine

not the common
nightingale of folklore

creator of sweet sounds
builder of homes
harbinger of hope

but a 7-year-old
named Amelia
hiding in a bomb shelter

singing "Let It Go"
from *Frozen*

a smiling child
with a golden halo

composed in the chaos
of a country

in the throes
of an unspeakable war

Slava Ukraini!

"We will never forgive.
  We will never forget."
—speech before Russian invasion

In olive green tees
worn in allegiance
to fellow soldiers

actor-comedian
President Zelensky
finds his true calling
on the streets of Kyiv

dodging missiles
and rocket fire
leading his people

never conceding defeat

Putin's Stain

on Ukraine
unprovoked war
and disinformation campaign

mouths agape
senses woke
atrocities rage

Putin's stain
remains

3.

Fame is a fickle food
upon a slippery plate.
—Emily Dickinson

Alfred Hitchcock: Never Woke

Notorious for practical jokes
"twist" endings and cameos

blonde women in eyeglasses
that fed his fetish

Hitch was frightened
by eggs and breakfast

That white round thing
without any hole

and the yellow yolk
how revolting

breaking and spilling
its liquid

but blood is jolly—
red, he said.

Purple Haze

"Music is my religion."
—Jimi Hendrix

Clothing his black persona
in sartorial costumes
and flamboyant showmanship

turning up the controls to max
using the petal and Fuzz Face
and the VOX Cry Baby wah-wah

fusing blues, jazz, rock, and soul
singer and composer Jimi Hendrix
playing with instrumental virtuosity

and controlled distortion
altered the course of modern
American psychedelic music

and at the age of 27
choked on his own vomit

Purple Rain: Epitaph for a Prince

1958–2016

Prince Rogers Nelson
born epileptic
but "cured by an angel"

weighed 112 pounds
stood five feet two
wore women's shoes

composed his first song
at the age of seven
on his father's piano

played basketball
in high school
trained in classical ballet

Sometimes seen with a cane—
leaping off speakers in high heels
caused him great pain

One of the greatest
musicians of his generation
he died at his Paisley Park home

in Minneapolis, Minnesota
from a fentanyl overdose
accidental, they say

Mitch

Rider-of-the-rails hobo
Robert Mitchum

learned early poetry
won't pay the bills

but journeyman
moviemaking will

Chain-smoking boozer
and doper

he went where
the money flowed

But try as he might to escape
the B-movie life he chose

he knew he must pay the piper
and he did—

succumbing to lung cancer
and the myth he built

4.

I dwell in possibility.
—Emily Dickinson

A Wild Shining

Owed to William Carlos Williams

So much depends
upon the way the wind
and the light come in
on a crisp October morning

transforming bright leaves
translucent and shining
igniting the dance

So much depends
upon the way the fox slips in
silent and still as a stone

then evaporates
before our eyes
red tail flashing

Fossil

"A republic, if you can keep it."
—Benjamin Franklin

Among the rubble
of the January breach

we find just
within our reach

relics
of our republic

and the country
we loved

Democracy

bedraggled and alone
draped in a tattered flag

sits on a street corner
eyes on the Dome

Home Boys, Oath Keepers
and Q-Anon let loose

lobbing rocks, tear gas
and The Big Lie
tightening the noose

Undeterred and resolute
she holds them at bay

her weapons Justice, Truth
and the American Way

Juneteenth

6/19/1865–6/19/1921

Celebrate
with Texas Pete Hot Sauce
hibiscus tea
Red Velvet Cake

Ruminate on slaves
laboring in cotton fields
news of emancipation
two years late

Think upon white supremacists
and insurrectionists
threatening to mock
and demolish democracy today

Once upon a Time

on a small lump of dirt called Earth
there lived a cult led by an outlier
named Trump, "the Terrible"
who coveted the tiny country of America
aka the USA

his strategy
to defeat The Big Three
Truth, Decency, and Democracy
and reign with Fake News
and The Big Lie

Accompanied by the Big Red Fox
and Kevin "the Killer" McCarthy
Jim "the Coyote" Jordan
and Rudy "the Rat" Giuliani

he met in the Meadows of Mark
for target practice
taking pot shots
at Mike "the Fence" Pence
and Liz "the Iron Maiden" Cheney
once allies but now deemed betrayers

At the Battle of Capitol Hill
he was defeated by the White Knight
(affectionately known
to his beloved public
as "Sleepy Joe"
because he never slept
never gave up
kept on fighting
biding his time
his mighty Sword of Justice
at his side)

That evil would-be czar
lost his Golden Helmet
and was banished
to the Never-Never Land
of Mar-a-Lago in Florida
where he lived
suspended in a Time capsule
gazing at the greens
wearing nothing but a long red tie
and a MAGA hat

Pandemic: 1918

"I had a little bird
   Its name was Enza
   I opened up the window
   and in-flu-enza!"
   —childhood skipping-rope rhyme
      from 1918

At first she thought he might be
"mounting the mare" of bloody flux
or coming down with the grippe

but in her gut she knew
it must be "the Blue Death"
of the pandemic that was raging

when her 14-year-old son
was struck with a high fever
skin turning dark indigo
then dying on the third day

In a daze she laid his body out
bathed it in camphor
dressed him in his Sunday best
placed a penny over each eye

stopped the clocks
turned the mirror backwards
waved a candle
over his body three times

said a blessing
climbed upon the table beside him
then lay down to rest

Eastertide: 2021

"Nothing is lost . . . everything is transformed."
—Antoine Lavoisier, 1774

The season turbulent and raw
with rains and hurricanes

burst on the scene
with an explosion of green

Stunned and reeling
practicing restraint

we saw irony and reason
in the sunshine

bathing
our pained faces

holding us
in its patient embrace

The Poetry of Redwoods

July 2022

The redwoods are burning

Talking heads tell us
the ancient redwoods
in the California forest
are in danger

We view the conflagration
ungainly space aliens
floating in smoke
holding hoses
placing sprinklers around
those venerable sentinels
witnesses to history

The redwoods are burning

Baldwin warned us
of the fire next time
Dylan rang the chimes

That grizzled poet
Robert Frost wrote
about a dark night coming

The redwoods are burning
The gyre is turning

I envision a landscape
of horror
a phantasmagoria of orange
trees lit from within
imploding like our country

ignited by fear
inflamed with fury
zero percent control

no escape
but to engage

About the Author

Nancy Dillingham is associate editor of the online poetry journal *Speckled Trout Review* and the coeditor of four anthologies of western North Carolina women writers. Her latest works are *Like Headlines: New and Selected Poems* and the chapbooks *Revelation, I Can't Breathe,* and *Vantages.* She lives in Asheville, NC.